With love
from ...
on your ...
anniversary

/ x

CW00336877

The Little Book of

LOVE POETRY

SUMMERSDALE

Summersdale Publishers Ltd
46 West Street
Chichester
West Sussex
PO19 1RP

www.summersdale.com

ISBN 1 84024 395 3

To Kitty

Contents

Introduction...9
Aphra Behn...13
William Blake..14
Anne Bradstreet..18
Emily Brontë..19
Elizabeth Barrett Browning.......................20
Robert Burns..26
Lord Byron...27
Thomas Campion..28
Thomas Carew...29
William Cartwright.......................................31
John Clare..32
Samuel Taylor Coleridge............................34
William Congreve...35
Henry Constable...36
George Crabbe..37
Emily Dickinson...38

John Donne..39
George Etheredge......................................40
Leigh (James Henry) Hunt.......................41
Robert Herrick...42
Victor Hugo..45
Ben Jonson...46
John Keats..50
Henry Wadsworth Longfellow..................52
George Meredith..53
Thomas Moore...54
Coventry Patmore.....................................56
Christina Rossetti......................................57
Dante Gabriel Rossetti.............................62
William Caldwell Roscoe...........................65
Edmond Rostand.......................................66
Sappho...67
Sir Walter Scott...68
William Shakespeare.................................69
Percy Bysshe Shelley.................................78

Sir Philip Sidney..81

Edmund Spenser..82

Robert Louis Stevenson......................................85

Edward Thomas..86

George Wither..87

William Wordsworth...88

Sir Thomas Wyatt..91

W. B. Yeats...93

Introduction

From the quickening heartbeat at the stirrings of passion, right through to the anguish of love lost, poetry is the perfect way to express different types of love, the form of the poem often reflecting the nature of the emotions. Alongside the heartfelt poetry of Shelley, this collection includes the wild and untamed poems of Emily Brontë and the measured, polished writing of Shakespeare.

Many of the writers represented in this volume write from experience, and with the remarkable love affairs they had it is not surprising that they were moved to write such stirring poetry. The most famous romantically linked poets are, of course, the Barrett Brownings. Robert had pledged his love to Elizabeth before he had even laid eyes on her, having been smitten by her poetry. After six years of an invalid's incarceration in her father's house, Elizabeth went to live with Robert in Italy where they had a son. Elizabeth died in Robert's arms after fifteen years of marriage. Their most beautiful love poems have been selected for this anthology.

At the other end of the spectrum are the tempestuous relationships of 'mad, bad and dangerous to know' Lord Byron, who was involved in a number of affairs with both men and women. The lustful poem 'To Ellen' included here gives an inkling of his insatiable desires.

Although the poets in this collection are long gone, their words of passion, infatuation, longing and tenderness have survived through the years because of the universal nature of love itself. Love and poetry can immortalise, and as Shakespeare wrote:
'So long as men can breathe, or eyes can see,
So long lives this, and this gives life to thee.'

The Dream

All trembling in my arms Aminta lay,
Defending of the bliss I strove to take;
Raising my rapture by her kind delay,
Her force so charming was and weak.
The soft resistance did betray the grant,
While I pressed on the heaven of my desires;
Her rising breasts with nimbler motions pant;
Her dying eyes assume new fires.
Now to the height of languishment she grows,
And still her looks new charms put on;
Now the last mystery of Love she knows,
We sigh, and kiss: I waked, and all was done.
'Twas but a dream, yet by my heart I knew,
Which still was panting, part of it was true:
Oh how I strove the rest to have believed;
Ashamed and angry to be undeceived!

Aphra Behn

The Question Answered

What is it men in women do require?
The lineaments of gratified desire.
Whatis it women do in men require?
The lineaments of gratified desire.

William Blake

I Laid Me Down Upon A Bank

I laid me down upon a bank
Where Love lay sleeping
I heard among the rushes dank
Weeping, Weeping.

Then I went to the heath and the wild
To the thistles and thorns of the waste
And they told me how they were beguil'd
Driven out, and compell'd to be chaste.

William Blake

Love's Secret

Never seek to tell thy love,
Love that never told can be;
For the gentle wind doth move
Silently, invisibly.

I told my love, I told my love,
I told her all my heart,
Trembling, cold, in ghastly fears,
Ah! she did depart.

Soon after she was gone from me,
A traveller came by,
Silently, invisibly:
He took her with a sigh.

William Blake

The Garden Of Love

I went to the Garden of Love,
And saw what I never had seen:
A Chapel was built in the midst,
Where I used to play on the green.

And the gates of this Chapel were shut,
And "Thou shalt not" writ over the door;
So I turn'd to the Garden of Love
That so many sweet flowers bore;

And I saw it was filled with graves,
And tombstones where flowers should be;
And Priests in black gowns were walking their round
And binding with briars my joys and desires.

William Blake

To My Dear And Loving Husband

If ever two were one, then surely we;
If ever man were loved by wife, then thee;
If ever wife was happy in a man,
Compare with me, ye women, if you can.
I prize thy love more than whole mines of gold,
Or all the riches that the East doth hold.
My love is such that rivers cannot quench,
Nor aught but love from thee give recompense.
Thy love is such I can no way repay;
The heavens reward thee manifold, I pray.
Then while we live in love let's so persevere
That when we live no more we may live ever.

Anne Bradstreet

Untitled

Come, the wind may never again
Blow as it now blows for us;
And the stars may never again shine as now they shine;
Long before October returns,
Seas of blood will have parted us;
And you must crush the love in your heart, and I the
love in mine!

Emily Brontë

Sonnet XLIII, From *The Portuguese*

How do I love thee? Let me count the ways.
I love thee to the depth and breadth and height
My soul can reach, when feeling out of sight
For the ends of Being and ideal Grace.
I love thee to the level of every day's
Most quiet need, by sun and candlelight.
I love thee freely, as men strive for Right;
I love thee purely, as they turn from Praise.
I love thee with the passion put to use
In my old griefs, and with my childhood's faith.
I love thee with a love I seemed to lose
With my lost saints, - I love thee with the breath,
Smiles, tears, of all my life! - and, if God choose,
I shall but love thee better after death.

Elizabeth Barrett Browning

Sonnet

Yet, love, mere love, is beautiful indeed
And worthy of acceptation. Fire is bright,
Let temple burn, or flax; an equal light
Leaps in the flame from cedar-plank or weed.
And love is fire. And when I say at need
I love thee . . . mark! . . . I love thee - in thy sight
I stand transfigured, glorified aright,
With conscience of the new rays that proceed
Out of my face toward thine. There's nothing low
In love, when love the lowest: meanest creatures
Who love God, God accepts while loving so.
And what I feel, across the inferior features
Of what I am, doth flash itself, and show
How that great work of Love enhances Nature's.

Elizabeth Barrett Browning

Sonnet

Indeed this very love which is my boast,
And which, when rising up from breast to brow,
Doth crown me with a ruby large enow
To draw men's eyes and prove the inner cost.
This love even, all my worth, to the uttermost,
I should not love withal, unless that thou
Hadst set me an example, shown me how,
When first thine earnest eyes with mine were crossed
And love called love. And thus, I cannot speak
Of love even, as a good thing of my own.
Thy soul hath snatched up mine all faint and weak,
And placed it by thee on a golden throne-
And that I love (O soul, we must be meek!)
Is by thee only, whom I love alone.

Elizabeth Barrett Browning

Sonnet

Belovèd, my Belovèd, when I think
That thou wast in the world a year ago,
What time I sat alone here in the snow
And saw no footprint, heard the silence sink
No moment at thy voice, but, link by link,
Went counting all my chains as if that so
They never could fall off at any blow
Struck by thy possible hand why, thus I drink
Of life's great cup of wonder! Wonderful
Never to feel thee thrill the day or night
With personal act or speech - nor even cull
Some prescience of thee with the blossoms white
Thou sawest growing! Atheists are as dull,
Who cannot guess God's presence out of sight.

Elizabeth Barrett Browning

Sonnet

And wilt thou have me fashion into speech
The love I bear thee, finding words enough,
And hold the torch out, while the winds are rough
Between our faces, to cast light on each?
I drop it at thy feet. I cannot teach
My hand to hold my spirit so far off
From myself . . . me . . . that I should bring thee proof
In words, of love hid in me out of reach.
Nay, let the silence of my womanhood
Commend my woman-love to thy belief,
Seeing that I stand unwon, however wooed,
And rend the garment of my life, in brief,
By a most dauntless, voiceless fortitude,
Lest one touch of this heart convey its grief.

Elizabeth Barrett Browning

Sonnet

If I leave all for thee, wilt thou exchange
And be all to me? Shall I never miss
Home-talk and blessing, and the common kiss
That comes to each in turn, nor count it strange,
When I look up, to drop on a new range
Of walls and floors, another home than this?
Nay, wilt thou fill that place by me which is
Filled by dead eyes too tender to know change?
That's hardest. If to conquer love, has tried,
To conquer grief, tries more, as all things prove
For grief indeed is love and grief beside.
Alas, I have grieved so I am hard to love.
Yet love me - wilt thou? Open thine heart wide,
And fill within, the wet wings of thy dove.

Elizabeth Barrett Browning

Had I A Cave

Had I a cave on some wild, distant shore,
Where the winds howl to the waves' dashing roar,
There would I weep my woes,
There seek my lost repose,
Till grief my eyes should close,
Ne'er to wake more!

Falsest of womankind' canst thou declare
All thy fond-plighted vows - fleeting as air!
To thy new lover hie,
Laugh o'er thy perjury;
Then in thy bosom try
What peace is there!

Robert Burns

To Ellen

Oh! might I kiss those eyes of fire,
A million scarce would quench desire:
Still would I steep my lips in bliss,
And dwell an age on every kiss;
Nor then my soul should sated be,
Still would I kiss and cling to thee:
Nought should my kiss from thine dissever;
Still would we kiss, and kiss forever,
E'en though the numbers did exceed
The yellow harvest's countless seed.
To part would be a vain endeavor:
Could I desist? Ah, never-never!

Lord Byron

Come, O Come

Come, O come, my life's delight,
Let me not in languor pine!
Love loves no delay; thy sight,
The more enjoyed, the more divine:
O come, and take from me
The pain of being deprived of thee!

Thou all sweetness dost enclose,
Like a little world of bliss.
Beauty guards thy looks: the rose
In them pure and eternal is.
Come, then, and make thy flight
As swift to me, as heavenly light.

Thomas Campion

Red And White Roses

Read in these Roses the sad story
Of my hard fate, and your owne glory.
In the White you may discover
The paleness of a fainting lover;
In the Red the flames still feeding
On my heart, with fresh wounds bleeding.
The White will tell you how I languish,
And the Red express my anguish;
The White my innocence displaying,
The Red my martyrdom betraying.
The frowns that on your brow resided,
Have those Roses thus divided.
Oh! let your smiles but clear the weather,
And then they both shall grow together.

Thomas Carew

Song: Mediocrity In Love Rejected

Give me more love or more disdain;
The torrid or the frozen zone
Bring equal ease unto my pain,
The temperate affords me none:
Either extreme of love or hate,
Is sweeter than a calm estate.

Give me a storm; if it be love,
Like Danaë in that golden shower,
I swim in pleasure; if it prove
Disdain, that torrent will devour
My vulture hopes; and he's possess'd
Of heaven, that's but from hell released.
Then crown my joys or cure my pain:
Give me more love or more disdain.

Thomas Carew

To Chloe, Who For His Sake
Wished Herself Younger

There are two births; the one when light
First strikes the new awaken'd sense;
The other when two souls unite,
And we must count our life from thence:
When you loved me and I loved you
The both of us were born anew.

Love then to us new souls did give
And in those souls did plant new powers;
Since when another life we live,
The breath we breathe is his, not ours:
Love makes those young whom age doth chill,
And whom he finds young keeps young still.

William Cartwright

Song

I wish I was where I would be
With love alone to dwell;
Was I but her or she but me
Then love would all be well.
I wish to send my thoughts to her
As quick as thoughts can fly;
But as the winds the waters stir
The mirrors change and flye.

John Clare

Love's Memories

Love's memories haunt my footsteps still
    Like ceaseless flowings of the river.
Its mystic depths say what can fill?
    Sad disappointment waits forever.

John Clare

The Exchange

We pledged our hearts, my love and I,
   I in my arms the maiden clasping;
   I could not tell the reason why,
   But, O, I trembled like an aspen.

Her father's love she bade me gain;
   I went, and shook like any reed!
   I strove to act the man - in vain!
We had exchanged our hearts indeed.

Samuel Taylor Coleridge

Song

See, see, she wakes, Sabina wakes!
And now the sun begins to rise;
Less glorious is the morn that breaks
From his bright beams than her fair eyes.

With light united, day they give,
But different fates ere night fulfill.
How many by his warmth will live!
How many will her coldness kill!

William Congreve

Sonnet

My lady's presence makes the roses red
Because to see her lips they blush for shame;
The lily's leaves, for envy, pale became,
For her white hands in them this envy bred.
The marigold the leaves abroad doth spread,
Because the sun's and her power is the same
The violet of purple colour came,
Dyed in the blood she made my heart to shed.
In brief, all flowers from her their virtue take;
From her sweet breath their sweet smells do proceed;
The living heat which her eyebeams do make
Warmeth the ground, and quickeneth the seed.
The rain, wherewith she watereth the flowers,
Falls from mine eyes, which she dissolves in showers.

Henry Constable

The Marriage Ring

The ring, so worn as you behold,
So thin, so pale, is yet of gold:
The passion such it was to prove -
Worn with life's care, love yet was love.

George Crabbe

Heart, We Will Forget Him

Heart, we will forget him!
You and I, tonight!
You may forget the warmth he gave,
I will forget the light.

When you have done, pray tell me,
That I may straight begin!
Haste! lest while you're lagging,
I may remember him!

Emily Dickinson

From 'The Anniversary'

All other things to their destruction draw,
Only our love hath no decay;
This, no tomorrow hath, nor yesterday,
Running it never runs from us away,
But truly keeps his first, last, everlasting day.

John Donne

To A Lady Asking Him
How Long He Would Love Her

It is not, Celia, in our power
To say how long our love will last;
It may be we within this hour
May lose those joys we now do taste:
The blessed, that immortal be,
From change in love are only free.

Then since we mortal lovers are,
Ask not how long our love will last;
But while it does, let us take care
Each minute be with pleasure passed:
Were it not madness to deny
To live because we're sure to die?

George Etherege

Jenny Kissed Me

Jenny kiss'd me when we met,
Jumping from the chair she sat in;
Time, you thief, who love to get
Sweets into your list, put that in!
Say I'm weary, say I'm sad,
Say that health and wealth have miss'd me,
Say I'm growing old, but add,
Jenny kiss'd me.

Leigh (James Henry) Hunt

To Electra

I dare not ask a kiss,
I dare not beg a smile,
Lest having that, or this,
I might grow proud the while.

No, no, the utmost share
Of my desire shall be,
Only to kiss that air,
That lately kissèd thee.

Robert Herrick

Upon The Nipples Of Julia's Breast

Have ye beheld (with much delight)
A red-rose peeping through a white?
Or else a cherry (double grac'd)
Within a lillie? Centre plac'd?
Or ever mark'd the pretty beam,
A strawberry shewes, halfe drown'd in cream?
Or seen rich rubies blushing through
A pure smooth pearl, and Orient too?
So like to this, nay all the rest,
Is each neat niplet of her breast.

Robert Herrick

Upon Julia's Clothes

When as in silks my Julia goes,
Then, then (me thinks) how sweetly flowes
The liquefaction of her clothes.

Next, when I cast mine eyes and see
That brave vibration each way free,
O how that glittering taketh me!

Robert Herrick

À Une Femme

Enfant! si j'étais roi, je donnerais l'empire,
Et mon char, et mon sceptre, et mon peuple à genoux,
Et ma couronne d'or, et mes bains de porphyre,
Et mes flottes, à qui la mer ne peut suffire,
        Pour un regard de vous!

Si j'étais Dieu, la terre et l'air avec les ondes,
Les anges, les démons courbés devant ma loi,
Et le profond chaos aux entrailles fécondes
L'éternité, l'espace, et les cieux, et les mondes,
        Pour un baiser de toi!

Victor Hugo

To Celia

Drink to me, only, with thine eyes,
And I will pledge with mine;
Or leave a kiss but in the cup
And I'll not look for wine.
The thirst that from the soul doth rise
Doth ask a drink divine;
But might I of Jove's nectar sup
I would not change for thine.

I sent thee late a rosy wreath,
Not so much honouring thee
As giving it a hope, that there
It could not wither'd be;
But thou thereon did'st only breath
And sent'st it back to me;
Since when it grows, and smells, I swear,
Not of itself, but thee.

Ben Jonson

A Vision Of Beauty

It was a beauty that I saw -
So pure, so perfect, as the frame
Of all the universe were lame
To that one figure, could I draw,
Or give least line of it a law:
A skein of silk without a knot !
A fair march made without a halt!
A curious form without a fault !
A printed book without a blot!
All beauty! - and without a spot.

Ben Jonson

Song

Have you seen but a bright lily grow
Before rude hands have touch'd it?
Have you mark'd but the fall of the snow
Before the soil has smutch'd it?
Have you felt the wool of beaver,
Or swan's down ever?
Or gave smelt o' the bud o' the brier,
Or the nard in the fire?
Or have ever tasted the bag of the bee?
O so white, O so soft, O so sweet is she!

Ben Jonson

Those Eyes

Ah! do not wanton with those eyes,
 Lest I be sick with seeing -
Nor cast them down, but let them rise,
 Lest shame destroy their being.

Ah! be not angry with those fires,
 For then their threats will kill me;
Nor look too kind on my desires,
 For then my hopes will spill me.

Ah! do not steep them in thy tears,
 For so will sorrow slay me;
Nor spread them as distraught with fears -
 Mine own enough betray me.

Ben Jonson

Sonnet

Bright star, would I were stedfast as thou art -
Not in lone splendour hung aloft the night
And watching, with eternal lids apart,
Like nature's patient, sleepless Eremite,
The moving waters at their priestlike task
Of pure ablution round earth's human shores,
Or gazing on the new soft fallen mask
Of snow upon the mountains and the moors -
No - yet still stedfast, still unchangeable,
Pillow'd upon my fair love's ripening breast,
To feel forever its soft fall and swell,
Awake forever in a sweet unrest,
Still, still to hear her tender-taken breath,
And so live ever - or else swoon to death.

John Keats

To Fanny

I cry your mercy - pity - love! - ay, love! -
Merciful love that tantalizes not,
One-thoughted, never-wandering, guileless love,
Unmask'd, and being seen - without a blot!
O! let me have thee whole - all - all - be mine!
That shape, that fairness, that sweet minor zest
Of love, your kiss - those hands, those eyes divine,
That warm, white, lucent, million-pleasured breast -
Yourself - your soul - in pity give me all,
Withhold no atom's atom or I die,
Or living on perhaps, your wretched thrall,
Forget, in the midst of idle misery,
Life's purposes - the palate of my mind
Losing its gust, and my ambition blind!

John Keats

The Evening Star

Lo! in the painted oriel of the West,
Whose panes the sunken sun incarnadines,
Like a fair lady at her casement, shines
The evening star, the star of love and rest!
And then anon she doth herself divest
Of all her radiant garments, and reclines
Behind the sombre screen of yonder pines,
With slumber and soft dreams of love oppressed.
O my beloved, my sweet Hesperus!
My morning and my evening star of love!
My best and gentlest lady! even thus,
As that fair planet in the sky above,
Dost thou retire unto thy rest at night,
And from thy darkened window fades the light.

Henry Wadsworth Longfellow

When I Would Image

When I would image her features,
Comes up a shrouded head:
I touch the outlines, shrinking;
She seems of the wandering dead.

But when love asks for nothing,
And lies on his bed of snow,
The face slips under my eyelids,
All in its living glow.

Like a dark cathedral city,
Whose spires, and domes, and towers
Quiver in violet lightnings,
My soul basks on for hours.

George Meredith

The Monopolist

If I were yonder wave, my dear,
And thou the isle it clasps around,
I would not let a foot come near
My land of bliss, my fairy ground!

If I were yonder conch of gold,
And thou the pearl within it placed,
I would not let an eye behold
The sacred gem my arms embraced!

If I were yonder orange tree,
And thou the blossom blooming there,
I would not yield a breath of thee,
To scent the most imploring air!

Thomas Moore

When I Loved You

When I loved you, I can't but allow
I had many an exquisite minute;
But the scorn that I feel for you now
Hath even more luxury in it!

Thus, whether we're on or we're off
Some witchery seems to await you;
To love you is pleasant enough,
But oh! 'tis delicious to hate you!

Thomas Moore

Across The Sky

Across the sky the daylight crept,
And birds grew garrulous in the grove,
And on my marriage-morn I slept
A soft sleep undisturb'd by love.

Coventry Patmore

Sonnet

I wish I could remember that first day,
First hour, first moment of your meeting me,
If bright or dim the season, it might be
Summer or Winter for aught I can say;
So unrecorded did it slip away,
So blind was I to see and to foresee,
So dull to mark the budding of my tree
That would not blossom yet for many a May.
If only I could recollect it, such
A day of days! I let it come and go
As traceless as a thaw of bygone snow;
It seemed to mean so little, meant so much;
If only now I could recall that touch,
First touch of hand in hand - Did one but know!

Christina Rossetti

Sonnet

O my heart's heart and you who are to me
More than myself myself, God be with you,
Keep you in strong obedience, leal and true
To him whose noble service setteth free,
Give you all good we see or can foresee,
Make your joys many and your sorrows few,
Bless you in what you bear and what you do,
Yea, perfect you as He would have you be.
So much for you; but what for me dear friend?
To love you without stint and all I can
Today, tomorrow, world without an end:
To love you much, and yet to love you more,
As Jordan at its flood sweeps either shore;
Since woman is the helpmeet made for man.

Christina Rossetti

Remember

Remember me when I am gone away,
Gone far away into the silent land;
When you can no more hold me by the hand
Nor I half turn to go, yet turning stay.
Remember me when no more day by day
You tell me of our future that you planned;
Only remember me; you understand
It will be late to counsel then or pray.
Yet if you should forget me for a while
And afterwards remember, do not grieve:
For if the darkness and corruption leave
A vestige of thought that once I had,
Better by far you should forget and smile
Than you should remember and be sad.

Christina Rossetti

Sonnet

Youth gone, and beauty gone if ever there
Dwelt beauty in so poor a face as this;
Youth gone and beauty, what remains of bliss?
I will not bind fresh roses in my hair,
To shame a cheek at best but little fair -
Leave youth his roses, who can bear a thorn -
I will not seek for blossoms anywhere,
Except such common flowers as blow with corn.
Youth gone and beauty gone, what doth remain?
The longing of a heart pent up forlorn,
A silent heart whose silence loves and longs;
The silence of a heart which sang its songs
While youth and beauty made a summer morn,
Silence of love that cannot sing again.

Christina Rossetti

Song

When I am dead, my dearest,
Sing no sad songs for me;
Plant thou no roses at my head,
Nor shady cypress tree:
Be the green grass above me
With showers and dewdrops wet;
And if thou wilt, remember,
And if thou wilt, forget.
I shall not see the shadows,
I shall not feel the rain;
I shall not hear the nightingale
Sing on, as if in pain;
And dreaming through the twilight
That doth not rise nor set,
Haply I may remember,
And haply may forget.

Christina Rossetti

Sudden Light

I have been here before,
But when or how I cannot tell:
I know the grass beyond the door,
The sweet keen smell,
The sighing sound, the lights around the shore.

You have been mine before -
How long ago I may not know:
But just when at that swallow's soar
Your neck turned so,
Some veil did fall,-I knew it all of yore.

Has this been thus before?
And shall not thus time's eddying flight
Still with our lives our love restore
In death's despite
And day and night yield one delight once more?

Dante Gabriel Rossetti

Silent Noon

Your hands lie open in the long fresh grass,
The finger-points look through like rosy blooms;
Your eyes smile peace. The pasture gleams and glooms
'Neath billowing skies that scatter and amass.
All round our nest, far as the eye can pass,
Are golden kingcup-fields with silver edge
Where the cow-parsley skirts the hawthorn-hedge.
'Tis visible silence still as the hourglass.
Deep n the sun-searched growths the dragonfly
Hangs like a blue thread loosened from the sky.
So this winged hour is dropt to us from above
Oh! clasp we to our hearts, for deathless dower,
This close-companioned inarticulate hour
When twofold silence was the song of love.

Dante Gabriel Rossetti

Willowwood

I sat with Love upon a woodside well,
  Leaning across the water, I and he;
Nor ever did he speak nor looked at me,
  But touched his lute wherein was audible
  The certain secret thing he had to tell:
Only our mirrored eyes met silently
In the low wave; and that sound seemed to be
The passionate voice I knew; and my tears fell.

And at their fall, his eyes beneath grew hers;
  And with his foot and with his wing feathers
He swept the spring that watered my heart's drouth.
  Then the dark ripples spread to waving hair,
  And as I stopped, her own lips rising there
Bubbled with brimming kisses at my mouth.

Dante Gabriel Rossetti

A Lover's Fear

Like a musician that with flying finger
Startles the voice of some new instrument,
And though he know that in one string are blent
All its extremes of sound, yet still doth linger
Among the lighter threads, fearing to start
The deep soul of that one melodious wire,
Lest it, unanswering, dash his high desire,
And spoil the hopes of his expectant heart;
Thus my mistress oft conversing, I
Stir every lighter theme with careless voice,
Gathering sweet music and celestial joys
From the harmonious soul o'er which I fly;
Yet o'er the one deep master-chord I hover,
And dare not stoop, fearing to tell – I love her.

William Caldwell Roscoe

From *Cyrano de Bergerac*

A kiss, when all is said, what is it?
An oath that's given closer than before;
A promise more precise; the sealing of
Confessions that till then were barely breathed;
A rosy dot placed on the i in loving;
A secret that is confined to a mouth and not to ears.

Edmond Rostand

Fragment 31

That man seems to me to be like a god, to
Sit so close to you and to hear your sweet voice
And your charming laughter – and all this, truly,
    Makes my heart tremble;

For I only, briefly, need glance at you to
Find my voice has gone and my tongue is broken,
And a flame has stolen beneath my skin, my
    Eyes can no longer

See, my ears are ringing, while drops of sweat run
Down my trembling body, and I've turned paler
Than a wisp of straw and it seems to me I'm
    Not far off dying.

Sappho

Love And The Rose

The rose is fairest when 'tis budding new,
And hope is brightest when it dawns from fears:
The rose is sweetest wash'd with morning dew,
And love is loveliest when embalm'd in tears.
O wilding rose, whom fancy thus endears,
I bid your blossoms in my bonnet wave,
Emblem of hope and love through future years!
Thus spoke young Norman, heir of Armandare
What time the sun arose on Vennachar's broad wave.

Sir Walter Scott

Sonnet

That time of year thou may'st in me behold
When yellow leaves, or none, or few, do hang
Upon those boughs which shake against the cold,
Bare ruined choirs, where late the sweet birds sang.
In me thou seest the twilight of such day
As after sunset fadeth in the west;
Which by and by black night doth take away,
Death's second self, that seals up all in rest.
In me thou seest the glowing of such fire,
That on the ashes of his youth doth lie,
As the death-bed whereon it must expire,
Consumed with that which it was nourished by.
This thou perceiv'st, which makes thy love more strong,
To love that well which thou must leave ere long.

William Shakespeare

Sonnet

Let me not to the marriage of true minds
Admit impediments. Love is not love
Which alters when it alteration finds,
Or bends with the remover to remove:
O, no; it is an ever-fixed mark,
That looks on tempests and is never shaken;
It is the star to every wandering bark,
Whose worth's unknown, although his height be taken.
Love's not Time's fool, though rosy lips and cheeks
Within his bending sickle's compass come;
Love alters not with his brief hours and weeks,
But bears it out even to the edge of doom.
If this be error and upon me prov'd,
I never writ, nor no man ever lov'd.

William Shakespeare

Sonnet

Thus can my love excuse the slow offense
Of my dull bearer when from thee I speed:
From where thou art why should I haste me thence?
Till I return, of posting is no need.
O, what excuse will my poor beast then find,
When swift extremity can seem but slow?
Then should I spur, though mounted on the wind,
In winged speed no motion shall I know:
Then can no horse with my desire keep pace;
Therefore desire, of perfect'st love being made
Shall neigh - no dull flesh - in his fiery race;
But love, for love, thus shall excuse my jade;
Since from thee going he went willful-slow,
Towards thee I'll run and give him leave to go.

William Shakespeare

Sonnet

Not marble, nor the gilded monuments
Of princes, shall outlive this powerful rhyme;
But you shall shine more bright in these contents
Than unswept stone, besmear'd with sluttish time.
When wasteful war shall statues overturn,
And broils root out the work of masonry,
Nor Mars his sword nor war's quick fire shall burn
The living record of your memory.
'Gainst death and all-oblivious enmity
Shall you pace forth; your praise shall still find room
Even in the eyes of all posterity
That wear this world out to the ending doom.
So, till the judgement that yourself arise,
You live in this, and dwell in lovers' eyes.

William Shakespeare

Sonnet

So are you to my thoughts as food to life,
Or as sweet-season'd showers are to the ground;
And for the peace of you I hold such strife
As 'twixt a miser and his wealth is found;
Now proud as an enjoyer, and anon
Doubting the filching age will steal his treasure;
Now counting best to be with you alone,
Then better'd that the world may see my pleasure:
Sometime all full with feasting on your sight,
And by and by clean starved for a look;
Possessing or pursuing no delight,
Save what is had or must from you be took.
Thus do I pine and surfeit day by day,
Or gluttoning on all, or all away.

William Shakespeare

Sonnet

Not from the stars do I my judgement pluck;
And yet methinks I have astronomy,
But not to tell of good or evil luck,
Of plagues, of dearths, or seasons' quality;
Nor can I fortune to brief minutes tell,
Pointing to each his thunder, rain and wind,
Or say with princes if it shall go well,
By oft predict that I in heaven find:
But from thine eyes my knowledge I derive,
And, constant stars, in them I read such art,
As truth and beauty shall together thrive,
If from thyself to store thou wouldst convert;
Or else of thee this I prognosticate:
Thy end is truth's and beauty's doom and date.

William Shakespeare

Sonnet

Shall I compare thee to a summer's day?
Thou art more lovely and more temperate:
Rough winds do shake the darling buds of May,
And summer's lease hath all too short a date:
Sometime too hot the eye of heaven shines,
And often is his gold complexion dimm'd;
And every fair from fair sometime declines,
By chance or nature's changing course untrimm'd;
But thy eternal summer shall not fade,
Nor lose possession of that fair thou ow'st;
Nor shall Death brag thou wander'st in his shade,
When in eternal lines to time thou grow'st;
So long as men can breathe, or eyes can see,
So long lives this, and this gives life to thee.

William Shakespeare

Sonnet

That thou hast her, it is not all my grief,
And yet it may be said I lov'd her dearly;
That she hath thee, is of my wailing chief,
A loss in love that touches me more nearly.
Loving offenders, thus I will excuse ye:
Thou dost love her, because thou knew'st I love her;
And for my sake even so doth she abuse me
Suffering my friend for my sake to approve her.
If I lose thee, my loss is my love's gain,
And losing her, my friend hath found that loss;
Both and each other, and I lose both twain
And both for my sake lay on me this cross:
But here's the joy; my friend and I are one;
Sweet flattery! then she loves but me alone.

William Shakespeare

Sonnet

Farewell! thou art too dear for my possessing,
And like enough thou know'st thy estimate:
The charter of thy worth gives thee releasing;
My bonds in thee are all determinate.
For how do I hold thee but by thy granting?
And for that riches where is my deserving?
The cause of this fair gift in me is wanting,
And so my patent back again is swerving.
Thyself thou gav'st, thy own worth then not knowing,
Or me, to whom thou gav'st it, else mistaking;
So thy great gift, upon misprision growing,
Comes home again, on better judgement making.
Thus have I had thee, as a dream doth flatter,
In sleep a king, but waking no such matter.

William Shakespeare

When Passion's Trance Is Overpast

When passion's trance is overpast,
If tenderness and truth could last,
Or live, whilst all wild feelings keep
Some mortal slumber, dark and deep,
I should not weep, I should not weep!

It were enough to feel, to see,
Thy soft eyes gazing tenderly,
And dream the rest - and burn and be
The secret food of fires unseen,
Couldst thou but be as thou hast been.

After the slumber of the year
The woodland violets reappear;
All things revive in field or grove,
And sky and sea, but two, which move
And form all others - life, and love.

Percy Bysshe Shelley

To –

One word is too often profaned
For me to profane it,
One feeling too falsely disdained
For thee to disdain it;
One hope is too like despair
For prudence to smother,
And pity from thee more dear
Than that from another.

I can give not what men call love,
But wilt thou accept not
The worship the heart lifts above
And the Heavens reject not –
The desire of the moth for the star,
Of the night for the morrow,
The devotion to something afar
From the sphere of our sorrow?

Percy Bysshe Shelley

Echoes And Memories

Music, when soft voices die,
Vibrates in the memory –
Odours, when sweet violets sicken,
Live within the sense they quicken .

Rose leaves, when the rose is dead,
Are heaped for the belovèd's bed;
And so thy thoughts, when thou art gone,
Love itself shall slumber on.

Percy Bysshe Shelley

Sonnet

With how sad steps, O moon, thou climb'st the skies;
How silently, and with how wan a face.
What, may it be that even in heav'nly place
That busy archer his sharp arrows tries?
Sure, if that long-with-love-acquainted eyes
Can judge of love, thou feel'st a lover's case;
I read it in thy looks; thy languished grace
To me that feel the like, thy state descries.
Then ev'n of fellowship, O moon, tell me
Is constant love deemed there but want of wit?
Are beauties there as proud as here they be?
Do they above love to be loved, and yet
Those lovers scorn whom that love doth possess?
Do they call virtue there ungratefulness?

Sir Philip Sidney

The Garden Of Beauty

Coming to kiss her lips (such grace I found),
Me seem'd I smelt a garden of sweet flow'rs
That dainty odours from them threw around,
For damsels fit to deck their lovers' bow'rs.
Her lips did smell like unto gilliflowers,
Her ruddy cheeks like unto roses red,
Her snowy brows like budded bellamoures,
Her lovely eyes like pinks but newly spread,
Her goodly bosom like a strawberry bed,
Her neck like to a bunch of cullambines,
Her breast like lilies ere their leaves be shed,
Her nipples like young blossom'd jessamines:
Such fragrant flow'rs do give most odourous smell,
But her sweet odour did them all excel.

Edmund Spenser

Love In Absence

Like as the culver on the bared bough
Sits mourning for the absence of her mate,
And in her songs sends many a wishful vow
For his return, that seems to linger late;
So I alone, now left disconsolate,
Mourn to myself the absence of my love,
And wandering here and there all desolate,
Seek with my plaints to match that mournful dove.
No joy of ought that under heaven doth hove
Can comfort me, but her own joyous sight,
Whose sweet aspect both god and man can move,
In her unspotted pleasance to delight:
Dark is my day whiles her fair light I miss,
And dead my life, that wants such lively bliss.

Edmund Spenser

My Love Is Like To Ice

My love is like to ice, and I to fire:
How comes it then that this her cold so great
Is not dissolved through my so hot desire,
But harder grows the more I her entreat!
Or how comes it that my exceeding heat
Is not allayed by her heart - frozen cold,
But that I burn much more in boiling sweat,
And feel my flames augmented manifold!
What more miraculous thing may be told
That fire, which all things melts, should harden ice,
And ice, which is congeal'd with senseless cold;
Should kindle fire by wonderful device!
Such is the power of love in gentle mind,
That it can alter all the course of kind.

Edmund Spenser

My Wife

Trusty, dusky, vivid, true,
With eyes of gold and bramble-dew,
Steel-true and blade-straight,
The great artificer
Made my mate.

Honour, anger, valour, fire;
A love that life could never tire,
Death quench or evil stir,
The mighty master
Gave to her.

Teacher, tender comrade, wife,
A fellow-farer true through life,
Heart-whole and soul-free
The august father
Gave to me.

Robert Louis Stevenson

Like The Touch Of Rain

Like the touch of rain she was
On a man's flesh and hair and eyes
When the joy of walking thus
Has taken him by surprise:

With the love of the storm he burns,
He sings, he laughs, well I know how,
But forgets when he returns
As I shall not forget her 'Go now.'

Those two shut a door
Between me and the blessed rain
That was never shut before
And will not open again.

Edward Thomas

Sonnet Upon A Stolen Kiss

Now gentle sleep hath closed up those eyes
Which, waking, kept my boldest thoughts in awe;
And free access unto that sweet lip lies,
From whence I long the rosy breath to draw.
Methinks no wrong it were, if I should steal
From those two melting rubies one poor kiss;
None sees the theft that would the theft reveal,
Nor rob I her of aught what she can miss:
Nay, should I twenty kisses take away,
There would be little sign I would do so;
Why then should I this robbery delay?
O, she may wake and therewith angry grow!
Well, if she do I'll back restore that one,
And twenty hundred thousand more for loan.

George Wither

Yes! Thou Art Fair

Yes! thou art fair, yet be not moved
    To scorn the declaration,
That sometimes I in thee have loved
    My fancy's own creation.

Imagination needs must stir:
    Dear maid, this truth believe,
Minds that have nothing to confer
    Find little to perceive.

Be pleased that nature made thee fit
    To feed my heart's devotion,
By laws to which all forms submit
    In sky, air, earth, and ocean.

William Wordsworth

What Heavenly Smiles!

What heavenly smiles! O Lady mine
Through my very heart they shine;
And, if my brow gives back their light,
Do thou look gladly on the sight;
As the clear Moon with modest pride
Beholds her own bright beams.
Reflected from the mountain's side
And from the headlong streams.

William Wordsworth

To –

Let other bards of angels sing,
Bright suns without a spot;
But thou art no such perfect thing:
Rejoice that thou art not!

Heed not tho' none should call thee fair:
So, Mary, let it be
If naught in loveliness compare
With what thou art to me.

True beauty dwells in deep retreats,
Whose veil is unremoved
Till heart with heart in concord beats,
And the lover is beloved.

William Wordsworth

Behold, Love, Thy Power

Behold, love, thy power how she despiseth!
My great pain how little she regardeth!
The holy oath, whereof she taketh no cure,
Broken she hath; and yet she bideth sure
Right at her ease and little she dreadeth.
Weaponed thou art, and she unarmed sitteth;
To the disdainful her life she leadeth,
To me spiteful without cause or measure,
       Behold, love.

I am in hold: if pity thee moveth,
Go bend thy bow, that stony hearts breaketh,
And with some stroke revenge the displeasure
Of thee and him, that sorrow doth endure,
And, as his lord, the lowly entreateth.
       Behold, love.

Sir Thomas Wyatt

A Renouncing Of Love

Farewell, love, and all thy laws forever:
Thy baited hooks shall tangle me no more;
Senec and Plato call me from thy lore,
To perfect wealth my wit for to endeavor.
In blind error when I did persever,
Thy sharp repulse, that pricketh ay so sore,
Hath taught me to set in trifles no store,
And scape forth, since liberty is lever.
Therefore, farewell: go trouble younger hearts,
And in me claim no more authority;
With idle youth go use thy property,
And thereon spend thy many brittle darts;
For hitherto though I have lost all my time,
Me lusteth no longer rotten boughs to climb.

Sir Thomas Wyatt

A Drinking Song

Wine comes in at the mouth
And love comes in at the eye;
That's all we know for truth
Before we grow old and die.
I lift the glass to my mouth,
I look at you, and I sigh.

W. B. Yeats

Brown Penny

I whispered, 'I am too young,'
And then, 'I am old enough';
Wherefore I threw a penny
To find out if I might love,
'Go and love, go and love, young man,
If the lady be young and fair.'
Ah, penny, brown penny, brown penny,
I am looped in the loops of her hair.

O love is the crooked thing
There is nobody wise enough
To find out all that is in it,
For he would be thinking of love
Till the stars had run away
And the shadows eaten the moon.
Ah, penny, brown penny, brown penny,
One cannot begin it too soon.

W. B. Yeats

The Pity Of Love

A pity beyond all telling
Is hid in the heart of love:
The folk who are buying and selling;
The clouds on their journey above;
The cold wet winds ever blowing;
And the shadowy hazel grove
Where mouse-grey waters are flowing
Threaten the head that I love.

W. B. Yeats

For a current publishing catalogue
and full listing of
Summersdale books,
visit our website:

www.summersdale.com